Moving On
Prayers for Relocating to A Retirement Community

Carlee L. Hallman
&
Howard W. Hallman

This book is available as an e-book from Amazon Kindle.

These prayers are also available on line at www.prayersformovingon.org.

The cover photo shows Carlee and Howard Hallman's garden at their retirement community.

Copyright © 2016 Carlee L. Hallman

All rights reserved.

ISBN-10:1537368923
ISBN-13:978-1537368924

To our daughters Beth and Joy
in appreciation of their love and support.

ACKNOWLEDGEMENTS

Biblical quotations are from the New Revised Standard Version (NRSV) unless otherwise noted.

Introduction

As we went through the decision to move and settle into a retirement community, prayer was our source of strength and inspiration. Our hope is that by sharing these prayers you may find similar strength and companionship for your journey.

At the age of 51, Carlee entered Wesley Seminary to become a United Methodist minister. She served small congregations in Maryland for eleven years. Upon retirement she was a volunteer chaplain at a local nursing home, wrote a devotional column for *Mature Years* magazine for a year and a half, and led a women's circle in the local church. In 2006, Abingdon Press published her book, *Abide With Me: Prayers for Life's Eventide*.

Howard's career has been in public service, dealing with such matters as housing, neighborhood improvement, manpower training, citizen participation, metropolitan governance, and world peace issues. He wrote nine books on these subjects. He has been active in local churches all his life, often serving on the social action committee. He recently published a book, *Living in God's Kingdom: Here and Now*.

We have two daughters and a grandson who have been supportive of us as we have entered a new phase of life.

As your journey brings you closer to God, may you find joy and peace. Isaiah 26:3: "Those of steadfast mind you keep in peace—in peace because they trust in you."

Contents

Introduction

Decision Time	1
Where to Go	9
Preparations	21
Neither Here nor There	31
Signed Up	43
Moving	55
Moved In	67
Fixing the Old House	77
Tests and Records	87
New Adventures	97
Getting Settled	107
Milestones	117
Closing	127
Scriptures Cited	139
Hymns	145

Decision Time

Jeremiah 33:3

Call to me and I will answer you, and will tell you great and hidden things that you have not known.

Let's Move

Her perspective

"It's time to move,"
I said to my husband.
"I don't have the energy
to clean this big house
or to prepare for company
like I used to.
It's time to move on."
"What do you have in mind?" he asked.
"A retirement home."
I'll think about it," he said.
You know, Lord, that since I retired
he is more connected than I am.
Besides the church,
he has music and softball.
I have my church circle
and writing groups.
I need more people my age.
Guide us in our decision.

John 16:13
When the Spirit of truth comes, he will guide you into all the truth; for he will not speak on his own, but will speak whatever he hears, and he will declare to you the things that are to come.

Hesitation

His perspective

Dear Lord, it's come up again.
My wife wants to move
to a retirement community.
We've talked about this
for several years
and have even looked at places.
I know it's a move
we should make some time,
but I'm not sure I'm ready to go.
It's overwhelming
when I think of all the things
we'll have to do:
decide where to go,
spruce up the house
before it goes on the market,
choose a realtor, show the house,
downsize, pack, and move.
Besides I'm comfortable
in this familiar setting.
Yet I recognize her need
for more friends and less housework.
In more than fifty years of our marriage
we've always resolved our differences.
Guide us as we work things out.

Psalm 31:3
You are indeed my rock and my fortress; for your name's sake lead me and guide me.

Patience

Her perspective

Dear God, my husband and I
are at standstill.
I'm ready to move
to a retirement community.
But he isn't. Not yet.
I think that it's a matter of inertia.
He's comfortable in our house
and keeps coming up with reasons
for not moving.
That's a change.
In our marriage he's always
been the adventurous one:
in picking vacation places,
willingness to change jobs
for a new opportunity,
even in buying a house
that stretched our resources.
At the same time he has a cautious streak
inherited from his father.
But when he decides something,
he moves ahead with determination.
I believe that he'll come around
if I give him a little more time.
So give me patience, dear Lord.

Romans 12:12
Rejoice in hope, be patient in suffering, persevere in prayer.

Health Concerns

His perspective

As you already know, O Lord,
my best friend had a stroke.
He's paralyzed on his right side
and confined to a wheel chair.
We played golf and went fishing together.
Now he's incapacitated.
It has given me a new perspective
on moving to a retirement community.
I look at myself in a full length mirror
and ask, "Could that be me
in a few years or even next month?"
Then I would be a burden to my wife.
Maybe she will be the first
to become ill, or break a hip.
We like to think that we are indestructible,
but we're not.
Yes, my wife is right.
It's time to move
before we have to.
I'll tell her.
She'll be glad.
Thanks for letting me talk
this through with you, dear Lord.

2 Samuel 22:29
Indeed, you are my lamp, O LORD,
the LORD lightens my darkness.

Second Thoughts

Her perspective

Dear Lord, my husband has
thought it through.
He's ready to move to a retirement community.
But now I'm not so sure.
When I think of the happy hours
on my backyard swing
in my lovely garden,
I wonder how I can ever leave.
Not to mention the antiques
I've collected over the years.
I know there wouldn't be a place
for all of them.
And my four sets of china,
including my grandmother's.
Yes, I know that Jesus sent out his disciples
without even a change of clothes,
and that our things shouldn't define us.
But it's memories, too.
It's a tough decision because
it's so final.

Mark 6:7-9
He called the twelve and began to send them out two by two, and gave them authority over the unclean spirits. He ordered them to take nothing for their journey except a staff; no bread, no bag, no money in their belts, but to wear sandals and not to put on two tunics.

The Big Decision

O Lord, we've finally decided.
We're going to sell our house
and move to a retirement community.
Deciding wasn't easy,
but after 50 years of marriage
we've learned how
to accommodate one another.
We don't talk about it a lot,
but love makes this possible.
Paul wrote,
love is patient and kind,
love doesn't insist on its own way,
love bears all things but never fails.
The Bible tells of your steadfast love
for the Hebrew people over the centuries.
May your steadfast love be with us
as we begin a new life.

1 Corinthians 13:4-8a
Love is patient; love is kind; love is not envious or boastful or arrogant or rude. It does not insist on its own way; it is not irritable or resentful; it does not rejoice in wrongdoing, but rejoices in the truth. It bears all things, believes all things, hopes all things, endures all things.

Where to Go

Romans 4:13
For the promise that he would inherit the world did not come to Abraham or to his descendants through the law but through the righteousness of faith.

Breaking the News

O Lord, today we told our children
that we are ready to move
to a retirement community.
One said, "It's about time."
The other one said,
"It's a good decision.
You'll get the care you need."
As if we were decrepit.
Then a flood of questions:
Where will you go?
When will you put
the house on the market?
Who will sell it for you?
How will you get rid
of the stuff you won't need?
Not a word about wanting something.
They also offered to help us
pack, move, and unpack.
We're grateful, Lord, for our children.
Lord, you have been good to us.

Psalm 127:3
Sons are indeed a heritage from the LORD, the fruit of the womb a reward.

Continuous Care

Dear Lord, now that we've decided to move,
we have to decide where to go--
so many choices, so much advice.
In our area there are several good
continuing care retirement communities.
We can start with independent living,
move to assisted living,
and finally to nursing home care,
twenty-four hours a day
for one or both of us.
That seems like a good idea.
It reminds us that
from birth, to maturity, to death,
we are under your continuous care.
Remind us again of your presence
as we enter another stage of life.

Psalm 23:1-3a
The LORD is my shepherd, I shall not want. He makes me lie down in green pastures; he leads me beside still waters; he restores my soul.

It's Not So Far

Dear Lord God,
I had a good laugh the other day.
I told our pastor
that we had looked at retirement communities
twelve and fifteen miles from our house,
and that that seemed a long way to move.
He chuckled and reminded me
that Abram was 75
when you told him to leave Haran
and take his family to the land of Canaan,
a distance of over 400 miles,
and he did.
I replied, "That may have been
a good move for Abram
because he was going
to the promised land."
Our pastor quickly responded,
"Maybe the retirement community
will be your promised land."

Genesis 12:1
Now the LORD said to Abram, "Go from your country and your kindred and your father's house to the land that I will show you."

Looking Forward

Lord, a friend told us that
going to a continuing care community
is like the woman who in succession
married a banker, actor, preacher, and undertaker.
One for the money, two for the show,
three to get ready, and four to go.
It's a lame old joke.
A neighbor told us that
he would never move
to a retirement home
because it's a place to die.
As if we could avoid death
by staying in one place.
I have no fear of dying.
I truly believe that there is
greater joy beyond the pale.
I look forward to being
with you in some new form,
reunited with loved ones,
and surrounded by abundant love.
Meanwhile, I know that
you will be with us
as we move.

Psalm 23:4a
Even though I walk through the darkest valley, I fear no evil; for you are with me.

Backyard Cathedral

O Lord, I'm sitting
on the backyard bench,
resting from raking leaves.
Across the yard
I see the swing
where my wife loves to sit
and write poetry.
I watch the bamboo grove
swaying in the breeze
at the back of the yard.
I look overhead
at six towering tulip poplar trees
that furnish shade in the summer.
It's like living
in a backyard cathedral.
For this we are grateful.
As we begin to think about
selling our house,
surely this will be
an attractive feature
to future buyers.
We ask you, Lord, to be with us
as we go through this time
of transition.

Psalm 9:10
And those who know your name put their trust in you, for you, O LORD, have not forsaken those who seek you.

Picking a Place

Lord, we've made our choice.
We're going to move to Evergreen Village,
a continuing care community of 1,200 residents.
It has a lovely campus.
We may even be able to have a garden plot.
There are six apartment buildings
for independent living,
one for assisted living,
and a health care center.
We visited the community center
with its fitness room and swimming pool.
We enjoyed lunch in the dining room.
We ate with a friendly couple
who warmly recommended the place.
There are lots of activities.
Almost too many, they warned us.
I think we'll be happy there.
Next month we'll select a specific unit.
Then we'll get on with the tasks
of selling our house, downsizing, and moving.
Thank you, Lord, for being with us.
Guide us as we go ahead.

Psalm 25:2a
O my God, in you I trust.

Choosing an Apartment

His Perspective

O Lord, we're ready to choose an apartment
at Evergreen Valley.
We're thinking of two bedrooms,
or one bedroom plus a den.
That will be larger than our apartment
when we got married:
a one-bedroom, third-floor walkup
with furniture from a second hand store.
As newlyweds we were happy there.
In between we've owned three houses
as our family grew and shrank:
a Cape Cod with three small bedrooms,
a big old six bedroom fix-up,
and a compact split level with three bedrooms.
Looking back, it wasn't the structure
but rather the quality of life
that made each house a home.
O Comforter and Sustainer, we ask your blessing
on our new apartment and our old age.

Numbers 6:24-26
The LORD bless you and keep you; the LORD make his face to shine upon you, and be gracious to you; the LORD lift up his countenance upon you, and give you peace.

Hymn: "Bless This House"

New Opportunity

Lord, our God, we have now
chosen an apartment.
It has a combined living-dining room,
bedroom, den, kitchen, and bathroom.
There is a balcony
that looks out over the trees.
We can see the sky
and changing patterns of clouds.
We grew up on the prairie
where we could see great distances.
It made us realize that there were many
opportunities for serving you.
Now moving to a retirement community
new opportunities for service are offered.
Open our eyes, Lord,
to new ways of service.

John 12:26
"Whoever serves me must follow me, and where I am, there will my servant be also. Whoever serves me, the Father will honor."

Spare Me

His Perspective

One of my friends warned me
that in some retirement communities
the female-male ratio is four to one:
lots of lonely widows looking for men.
"You haven't had this good picking
since high school," he joked.
"Not me," I replied "I'm a one woman man."
"Then if you become a widower,"
he went on,
"you'll be even more vulnerable."
Spare me, O Lord! Spare me!
And spare my wife.
Let her be the survivor.

Genesis 15:15
As for yourself, you shall go to your ancestors in peace; you shall be buried in a good old age.

Places for Prayer

Sitting on our swing,
my husband and I
are enjoying the backyard
and saying goodbye
to the birds, the bushes, flowers,
and the fountain he put in.
We will miss this quiet place, Lord.
The apartment grounds
of the retirement community
are public space.
You needed time apart for prayer.
Help us to find new places
in nature to be alone
to talk with you.

Matthew 14:23a
And after he had dismissed the crowds, he went up the mountain by himself to pray.

Mark 1:35
In the morning, while it was still very dark, he got up and went out to a deserted place, and there he prayed.

Preparations

Exodus 23:20
I am going to send an angel in front of you, to guard you on the way and to bring you to the place that I have prepared.

Realtor's Advice

Lord, now that we've selected a new apartment,
we're putting our house on the market.
We've decided on the realtor
who helped our daughter
sell her house and buy another.
He noted positive features of our house:
New roof, modern appliances, new windows,
good furnace and air-conditioning,
and close to a good school.
Then he suggested that
we remove the wallpaper in the dining room,
take up the wall-to-wall carpeting,
and refinish the hardwood floors.
"That's what younger buyers prefer," he said.
Amazing! I was glad to have carpeting
and not have to dust around rugs
like my grandmothers did.
Whatever changes we decide on,
O God of my childhood,
youth, middle age, and now old age,
we can rely on you to be the same.

Malachi 3:6
For I the LORD do not change; therefore you, O children of Jacob, have not perished.

Downsizing

O Lord God, in getting ready to move,
our newest challenge
is downsizing.
How to reduce the contents
of an eight room house
to a three room apartment.
We have to decide
what to take,
what to sell, give away,
or throw out.
These things,
saved through the years,
have many memories.
Help us to keep our eyes
on eternal values
as we let go of these
temporal things.

Deuteronomy 33:27 (KJV)
The eternal God is your refuge, and underneath are the everlasting arms.

Preparing the House

Father God, the realtor said
that in preparing to show the house
to potential buyers,
we should make the house
look as impersonal as possible.
The refrigerator magnets
have gone into a box.
We have stashed things
in cupboards, drawers,
and under the sofa and bed.
It's hard to remember
where things are
when we need them.
I can't wait to get settled
in our new place,
where we can put everything out
on tables and counters.
Are you laughing, Father?
Bare surfaces
just don't agree with me.

Ecclesiastes 3:11
He has made everything suitable for its time; moreover he has put a sense of past and future into their minds, yet they cannot find out what God has done from the beginning to the end.

Lightening the Load

After all these years,
I am finally getting rid
of papers I have saved
from grade school and college.
I hate to see them go, Lord,
but the essence of them
is stored in memory.
Letting go of the old
leaves room for new possibilities.
Lead me forward, Lord,
that each new day
will be another memorable day
lived in your presence.

Psalm 16:11
You show me the path of life. In your presence there is fullness of joy; in your right hand are pleasures forevermore.

Cleaning Out the Garage

His Perspective

O Lord Jesus, I'm starting
to clean out the garage
and sort through my memories.
There's stuff I'll never use
in our retirement home.
Snow shovels: I've worn out a half dozen
in fifty-five years of home ownership.
When we were young, my wife
insisted on shoveling snow
to save me from a heart attack.
I soon took over and have survived
more than fifty winters.
The lawn mower: no more grass cutting.
Garden tools: if we get a garden plot
at Evergreen Village,
they have community tools.
My old hand-made workbench:
On it I made a toy box for my daughters.
There I taught my grandson
how to saw wood and hammer nails.
I've even used the wood vise
to hold pickle jar tops.
O Master Carpenter,
I thank you for the experience
of working with my hands.

Deuteronomy 2:7a
Surely the LORD your God has blessed you in all your undertakings.

Letting Go

We will have less room
in our retirement apartment.
But, Lord, it is hard to let go
of the drawings
and other artwork
of our children.
Our children laugh at me
for saving their things.
I will still hide a few
but many will be let go.
The children are grown now.
They are not savers.
They may have a few things
from their own children's schooling,
but not much.
Each age has its challenges
and special gifts.
Help me to see
the treasure to be found
in each special day.

Psalm 143:5
I remember the days of old,
I think about all your deeds,
I meditate on the works of your hands.

Anxious

With our house now on the market, Lord,
showing it is getting to be old hat.
When we learn that someone is coming,
we have a drill: turn on all the lights,
put out the lock box, and leave.
It's hard to be ready all the time.
I'm afraid to start baking cookies
or begin a sewing project.
Our realtor is still telling us that
in order to sell the house
we need to take up the wall-to-wall carpeting
and refinish the floors.
It's a big job, Lord.
We'll have to think about it.
Give us wisdom and strength.

Job 12:13
"With God are wisdom and strength; he has counsel and understanding."

Psalm 46:1
God is our refuge and strength, a very present help in trouble.

Hymn: "Great Is Thy Faithfulness"

Survival Mode

Father God, it's not only
my aches and pains,
but my husband's blood pressure
that causes concern.
With no immediate buyers,
we're thinking of lowering
the price of the house
so that it sells quickly.
How much will be enough?
The tension is killing us.
Lord, we need your arms around us,
but how can you protect us
from ourselves?
Give us peace, Father, and rest.
We can't manage without you.

Matthew 11:28
"Come to me, all you that are weary and are carrying heavy burdens, and I will give you rest."

Hymn: "Leave It There"

Neither Here nor There

Job 28:12
"But where can wisdom be found? And where is the place of understanding?

Psalm 40:1
I waited patiently for the LORD; he inclined to me and heard my cry.

Worry! Worry! Worry!

O Lord Jesus, with our house
now on the market
we've scheduled movers and
a sale for extra household goods.
Now new worries begin.
Will we sell the house promptly,
so the movers can come as scheduled,
and the sale of extra household goods
be held as scheduled after that?
It could all go smoothly,
or we might have to reschedule
and reschedule.
Lord, help me to remain calm
and enjoy each day as it comes.
Your will be done. Amen.

Luke 12:25-26
"And can any of you by worrying add a single hour to your span of life? If then you are not able to do so small a thing as that, why do you worry about the rest?"

Hymn: "What a Friend We Have in Jesus"

Change

It's a beautiful morning, Lord.
The neighborhood is quiet.
How different it will be
to live on the seventh floor.
Here I go out in my robe
to get the paper.
There I only have to open the door
and find it on the floor.
It takes me awhile in the morning
to be ready to see other people.
I need a quiet time with you,
a time to read the paper,
and work the crossword puzzle.
It will be an adjustment, Lord.

Lamentations 3:25-26
The LORD is good to those who wait for him, to the soul who seeks him. It is good that one should wait quietly for the salvation of the LORD.

Not Perfect

Gracious God, you know
I have not been a tidy housekeeper,
but to be graded by realtors as "average,"
when I have been zealous in cleaning
in order to sell the house,
is a blow.
No telling what they would say
about my usual standard.
I try to keep things healthy,
and I make an extra effort
when company is coming.
I wonder what others have thought
all these years.
Have mercy, Gracious God.

Psalm 119:96
I have seen a limit to all perfection, but your commandment is exceedingly broad.

Scent

Gracious Lord, now I have packed
all my little bottles of perfume.
Some I have had a long time.
In our church, we have been advised
against wearing perfume in public,
since people with allergies
may be made uncomfortable.
Sometimes I wear perfume
when I'm going to stay home.
You allowed a woman
to pour ointment on your head
in preparation for your burial.
I wonder if they have rules
about this in our retirement home?

Proverbs 27:9a
Perfume and incense make the heart glad.

Matthew 26:6-7
Now while Jesus was at Bethany in the house of Simon the leper, a woman came to him with an alabaster jar of very costly ointment, and she poured it on his head as he sat at the table.

Flowers

This morning, Lord,
the perfume of an Easter lily
in the kitchen reminded me
that you noticed flowers,
prayed in the Garden of Gethsemane,
and met Mary Magdalene in a garden.
Flowers offer constant inspiration
as each variety blooms,
one after the other.
Thank you, Lord,
that we have been assigned a garden
at our new retirement home
even before we have signed up
to live there.

Luke 12:27
"Consider the lilies, how they grow: they neither toil nor spin; yet I tell you, even Solomon in all his glory was not clothed like one of these."

Hymn: "In the Garden"

Still Waiting

Monday morning
and another weekend has gone by,
and the house is not sold.
Yet, Lord, when I put my trust in you,
I know all will be well,
though not necessarily
in the way we expected.
You are with us
to give us strength.
Hold us up
during this time
of uncertainty.

Psalm 37:7a
Be still before the LORD, and wait patiently for him, do not fret over those who prosper in their way.

Isaiah 40:31a
But those who wait for the LORD shall renew their strength.

Loaned Treasures

Lord, we are packing things up
to save for the sale after we move.
They don't allow lighted candles
in the retirement community,
so candle holders, candles, and matches
are packed away.
There won't be room for many figurines,
coffee table books, and extra dishes.
You know, Lord, how these things
have enriched our lives.
We hope whoever buys them will enjoy them, too.
Thank you, Lord, for loaning them to us.

Matthew 6:19-21
"Do not store up for yourselves treasures on earth, where moth and rust consume and where thieves break in and steal; but store up for yourselves treasures in heaven, where neither moth nor rust consumes and where thieves do not break in and steal. For where your treasure is, there your heart will be also."

Spring Fever

O God of Creation,
on such a beautiful day,
I can't stay inside
waiting for the phone to ring.
I do go in and check
the answering machine
and computer
every now and then.
I don't want to miss a call
from someone wanting to see the house,
but there are only so many beautiful days,
and it may be my last chance
to sit on the swing in the garden.
I wouldn't want to miss
such a wonderful spring day.
Thank you, God, for spring days.

Isaiah 61:11
For as the earth brings forth its shoots, and as a garden causes what is sown in it to spring up, so the Lord GOD will cause righteousness and praise to spring up before all the nations.

Spring Gifts

I look through the window
and see feathery new leaves
backlighted by the sun.
Dogwoods blossom,
azaleas flame with color,
spring is fully here.
Lord God, can you be far away,
when your handiwork
is everywhere?
Next year these will bloom,
but I'll have to find new places
to talk with you.
Father, thank you for flowers
and for always being with me.

James 1:17 (KJV)
Every good gift and every perfect gift is from above, and cometh down from the Father of lights, with whom is no variableness, neither shadow of turning.

Signed Up

Luke 14:28
"For which of you, intending to build a tower, does not first sit down and estimate the cost, to whether he has enough to complete it?"

Signing Up

Today we signed
our final commitment
for the apartment
at the retirement village.
We have a loan from the corporation
which we hope will last
until the house is sold.
It's a worry, Lord.
Give us of your Spirit
that we may remain calm.
Hold us up, whatever happens.

Acts 2:17
"In the last days it will be," God declares, "that I will pour out my Spirit upon all flesh, and your sons and your daughters shall prophesy, and your young men shall see visions, and your old men shall dream dreams."

Hymn: "Spirit of God, Descend upon My Heart"

Moving Soon

We are moving next week,
whether or not the house is sold.
My church circle meets today, as usual.
The neighbors go on about their business.
Moving seems so monumental to us.
It's exciting to look forward to new things.
But, Father, will anyone miss us?
We will keep coming to church here,
and I will continue to come to meetings.
Still, even though we are the ones leaving,
without your presence, Father,
we would feel abandoned.
Your presence holds us up
wherever we go.

Psalm 139:9-10
If I take the wings of the morning and settle at the farthest limits of the sea, even there your hand shall lead me, and your right hand shall hold me fast.

Creating Order

This morning
as I emptied the dishwasher
in our house,
I knew where everything went.
When we move,
my mind will be a jumble
trying to remember
where we put things.
O Gracious Father,
you created the world
with a certain order;
the plants in the garden
grow a certain way.
In my new kitchen
it will take me awhile to decide
where things should go.
Remember me, Father,
as I struggle with new ways.

Genesis 1:1 (KJV)
In the beginning God created the heavens and the earth.

Psalm 119:27
Make me understand the way of your precepts, and I will meditate on your wondrous works.

Quiet Time

Sitting on my swing,
perhaps for the last time.
I am hidden by bamboo
on the back and sides,
and by the trees and house on the front.
Will I find a sheltered spot
in our new location
to be with you, Lord?
How can I talk with you
with people walking by?
It's hard to break in
to smile and say, "Hello,"
or ignore them entirely.
Would people understand?
I doubt it, Lord.
How I shall miss this place
where we can be alone.

Mark 6:31
He said to them, "Come away to a deserted place all by yourselves and rest a while." For many were coming and going, and they had no leisure even to eat.

Gardens

Father, you created the Garden of Eden
and walked in it with Adam and Eve.
Jesus talked with you
in the Garden of Gethsemane.
Gardens inspire
and remind us of your presence.
Now I am saying, "Good-bye," to the garden
at our house.
Next week we will have a new plot
to dig up and plant.
Great Father, I shall miss this place
where we have been together
so many times.
Lead me forward.
Help me let go of the past.

Genesis 3:8a
They heard the sound of the LORD God walking in the garden at the time of the evening breeze.

Matthew 26:36
Then Jesus went with them to a place called Gethsemane, and he said to his disciples, "Sit here while I go over there and pray."

April 1, Waiting

It's April Fools' Day, Lord.
I told my husband
that there was a mouse
under my desk.
When he was down
looking for it,
I said, "April Fool."
We laughed.
It's been years
since I've caught him.
We've been so preoccupied
with moving that he wasn't thinking.
Your quip about the camel
and the eye of the needle
must have given the disciples
a chuckle even as they got the message.
Light moments lift us
in heavy times, Lord.
Thank you for humor.

Mark 10:25
"It is easier for a camel to go through the eye of a needle than for someone who is rich to enter the kingdom of God."

Gentle Rain

Thank you, Lord,
for the gentle rain
that fell yesterday.
It refreshed the flowers.
After many sunny days
a rainy day is like a blessing.
The iris leaves are bent
with glowing beads of water.
The petals of the primrose glisten.
Thank you, Lord,
for your continued care.
I want the garden
to be doing well
for the new owners.

Psalm 147:7-8
Sing to the LORD with thanksgiving; make melody to our God on the lyre. He covers the heavens with clouds, prepares rain for the earth, makes grass grow on the hills.

Hymn: "Joyful, Joyful, We Adore Thee"

Aches and Pains

O Lord God,
you know my knee hurts
and now my shoulder aches.
I know these will go away
once the house is sold.
I'm sorry, Lord,
that I can't seem to
rest in your care.
If I could, I expect
I would be fine.
Help me, Lord,
to let go
and let you handle things.

Isaiah 26:3 (KJV)
Thou wilt keep him in perfect peace, whose mind is stayed on thee: because he trusteth in thee.

Procession

Another beautiful day, Lord of Creation!
Yellow iris
and red and yellow roses bloom.
Purple irises have had their day.
Columbines, planted last year,
are starting to bloom
How I will miss
this succession of flowers
when we move.
But it will be fun
to begin in a new plot,
and beautiful days
will unfold in our new garden
and community, too.
Thank you, Lord,
for the wonders of creation.

Song of Solomon 2:12
The flowers appear on the earth; the time of singing has come, and the voice of the turtledove is heard in our land.

Moving

Genesis 12:4b
Abram was seventy-five years old when he departed from Haran.

Monday

This is the week we will move
whether the house is sold or not.
Our daughters will help
with packing.
We have decided
to take the house off the market
and remove the carpets
and wall paper.
After our furniture is removed,
people will be able
to see the house better.
Then we hope it will sell
before too long.
We have a loan until then.
We are counting on you, Lord,
to see us through.

Hebrews 13:5-6
Keep your lives free from the love of money, and be content with what you have; for he has said, "I will never leave you or forsake you." So we say with confidence, "The Lord is my helper; I will not be afraid. What can anyone do to me?"

Hymn: "How Firm a Foundation" verse 2

More Aches and Pains

O Lord, now I've done it.
As I lifted the glass table top
on the deck to wash it,
my back wrenched.
I've washed that top many times.
It's not that heavy,
but it just caught my back today.
I continued trying to paint trim
with my daughter,
but I wasn't much help.
She got it done.
We will move soon and I am a mess.
Lord, how could this happen?
In spite of it,
we are going out to dinner
with a friend, who is so thoughtful.
Thank you, Lord, for those
who care in the midst of disaster.

1 Corinthians 12:26
If one member suffers, all suffer together with it; if one member is honored, all rejoice together with it.

Packing

My daughters are packing everything
that will move with us.
Thank you, Great God,
for our wonderful daughters.
They know just what to do.
I am keeping out of the way—
by packing little things and cleaning.
The movers come tomorrow.
Some things will stay here
for the sale after we move.
I try to sort things
before they get packed.
The marvel is
that we all get along so well
under the strain.
Thank you, Great God
for your guidance and love
in the thick of things.

Psalm 31:3
You indeed are my rock and my fortress; for your name's sake lead me and guide me.

Hymn: "Lead On, O King Eternal"

Moving Day Tomorrow

Lord, we sleep here in our house tonight
and in our apartment tomorrow night.
The moving company
will make the bed,
hang pictures,
and put things away in the kitchen.
We will sleep in our guest room tonight
since that furniture
will later go on sale.
Moving is an adventure, Lord.
If my back didn't hurt
everything would be fine.
Give me strength, Lord.

Isaiah 30:15a
For thus said the Lord GOD, the Holy One of Israel: In returning and rest you shall be saved; in quietness and in trust shall be your strength.

Moving Day

I was looking forward
to the excitement of moving,
but instead of enjoying it,
I have a sore back
and moving around is painful.
My daughters have packed for two days
and are still packing
as the moving men carry things out.
Is this pain psychological?
I have always liked change,
but maybe I don't know myself
as well as I thought.
You, Lord, are my relief and joy
at all times, even in pain.
Thank you, Lord, for your continuing presence.

Matthew 28:20b
"And remember, I am with you always, to the end of the age."

Hymn: "Leaning on the Everlasting Arms"

Saying "Good-bye"

This neighborhood
has been different
from other neighborhoods
we have lived in.
The people here lead
separate lives.
They don't get together.
We organized a couple of block parties
when we first moved here,
but no one continued it.
I hope to see our immediate neighbors
or will leave a note
to say "good-bye"
and give our new address
in case something comes up
that we need to know.
Watch over all of us, Lord.
We need your care.

Luke 10:27
He answered, "You shall love the Lord your God with all your heart, and with all your soul, and with all your strength, and with all your mind; and, your neighbor as yourself."

Bird Feeders

Father God, our bird feeders
will have to stay
with the house
or be given away.
Our seventh floor apartment
with a balcony
is no place for them.
I have seen bird feeders
on the lawn of these apartments.
I wonder who takes care of them.
I know you will feed them, Father.
Thank you for birds
and for your care.

Matthew 6:26a
"Look at the birds of the air; they neither sow nor reap nor gather into barns, and yet your heavenly Father feeds them."

Our Canoe

There at the side of the yard
sits our old canoe.
It's heavy compared to today's models
and too heavy for us to carry anymore.
We enjoyed using it in streams and lakes
when we were young.
We still have the paddles, life vests,
and seat cushions to go with it
in the garage.
We are grateful, Lord,
that our grandson decided to take it
and store it at his mother's house.
We hope he will enjoy it
as we did. Being close to the water
is a special reminder
of your presence with us.
It speaks of your calming the water
and of the Holy Spirit within.

Luke 8:24
They went to him and woke him up, shouting, "Master, Master, we are perishing!" And he woke up and rebuked the wind and the raging waves; they ceased, and there was a calm.

Acts 2:38
Peter said to them, "Repent, and be baptized every one of you in the name of Jesus Christ so that your sins may be forgiven; and you will receive the gift of the Holy Spirit."

Presence

Creative God, I have always enjoyed
new adventures.
But this time it's hard to let go
of the familiar.
This time it's so final.
It's looking forward
to smaller space
rather than larger.
Having more people around
will be wonderful,
but it will mean
few outdoor places of solitude
to talk with you, O Creative God.
Yet sharing your Spirit with others
is part of knowing your presence.
Lead me as I look for you
in new places and people.

Romans 8:37-39
No, in all these things we are more than conquerors through him who loved us. For I am convinced that neither death, nor life, nor angels, nor rulers, nor things present, nor things to come, nor powers, nor height, nor depth, nor anything else in all creation, will be able to separate us from the love of God in Christ Jesus our Lord.

**Hymn: "Holy, Holy, Holy! Lord God Almighty"
(verse 4)**

Moved In

Genesis 13:18
So Abram moved his tent, and came and settled by the oaks of Mamre, which are at Hebron; and there he built an altar to the LORD.

1st Day, New Apartment

Ah Lord! We are here.
We have spent our first night
in our new home.
A little rose plant and a welcome card
from our floor leader
was placed on the shelf outside our door,
along with a copy
of rules and regulations.
There will be a floor meeting
on Monday. They say that's the place
to get any issues addressed.
Should I tell them
about our stopped up sink
and the repair man who unintentionally
shot black goo all over cabinets and floor
from one end of the kitchen to the other?
I wiped it off the cabinets.
He wiped the floor, which I later washed.
He said he was having a bad day!
Thank you, Lord,
for letting me get it off my chest.

Philippians 4:8
Finally, beloved, whatever is true, whatever is honorable, whatever is just, whatever is pure, whatever is pleasing, whatever is commendable, if there is any excellence and there is anything worthy of praise, think about these things.

Hymn: "Nobody Knows the Trouble I've Seen"

Day 2, In Our Apartment

Gracious God, its Sunday,
a day of rest.
We made it to Sunday school
in our old neighborhood,
and I nearly went to sleep.
I felt more awake
in the church service
which had special music.
After the service
we visited with friends.
It's a little drive,
but we will keep attending
as long as possible.
We could go to church
in this retirement community
or at a church nearby.
Gracious God, thank you
for always being with us.

Psalm 95:2
Let us come into his presence with thanksgiving; let us make a joyful noise to him with songs of praise!

Moved In

Here we are, Lord,
in our new apartment.
The movers put everything
away in closets
and kitchen cabinets.
The furniture is placed
like it was in our house.
The space is smaller,
but the essentials are here.
It will take a while
to get used to living here,
not only in this apartment,
but with new people around.
Your presence, Lord, is our assurance
that we will adjust
and find others who share your Spirit.

1 John 4:13
By this we know that we abide in him and he in us, because he has given us of his Spirit.

Hymn: "God Will Take Care of You"

Reorganization

Ah Lord of Grace and Beauty,
Ah Lord of Peace and Harmony,
this place is a mess.
The movers and helpers
put things away.
Now I must reorganize
and find places for some things
and get rid of others.
We are going back and forth
between house and apartment
to exchange things we don't want
for things we do want.
Getting things in order
will be a challenge
but will be a relief in the end.

2 Corinthians 13:11
Finally, brothers and sisters, farewell. Put things in order, listen to my appeal, agree with one another, live in peace; and the God of love and peace will be with you.

Satisfied

We look forward to the meals here, Father.
The food and the company are good.
We have choices of food
and whether to sit with others or alone.
They give such big portions of food
that we take some home in boxes
to eat the next day.
I don't know when we'll eat the food
we bring home.
We are getting to know new people.
Everyone is so friendly.
Thank you, Father, for good food
and friendly people.

Acts 14:16-17
"In past generations he allowed all the nations to follow their own ways; yet he has not left himself without a witness in doing good---giving you rains from heaven and fruitful seasons; and filling you with food and your hearts with joy."

Eating Out

Every evening we go to dinner
in the dining room, Lord.
We could eat in our apartment
if I wanted to cook.
We could eat our main meal at noon,
but we like it at night.
Being new, we eat with different people
as we are assigned
when we enter the dining room.
We could also arrange to meet friends.
The food is good,
and there are many choices.
We can also take soup and a roll
or left-over food back with us
for lunch the next day.
We do not waste food.
You gave us the example, Lord,
when you had the disciples gather up
the remains after feeding the 5,000.
We are thankful for good food
and new friends.
Thank you, Lord.

Mark 6:42-44
And all ate and were filled; and they took up twelve baskets full of broken pieces and of the fish. Those who had eaten the loaves numbered five thousand men.

Hymn: "Praise God, from Whom All Blessings Flow"

Helpless

O Lord, we wait your word.
We are in limbo,
waiting for the house to sell
so that we can pay
for the apartment we've moved into
in the retirement community.
We feel helpless,
not in control.
We put ourselves in your hands, Lord.
Then whatever happens,
we will be all right.

Romans 8:26
Likewise the Spirit helps us in our weakness; for we do not know how to pray as we ought, but that very Spirit intercedes with sighs too deep for words.

Tuesday

Today I spent time
at our daughter's house
while my husband
worked on the garage.
Later after we went
back to our apartment,
our daughter came by
to hang some of our pictures
before going on an outing.
We ate dinner in our apartment,
eating up leftovers
from the large meals
they serve here.
We give you thanks
for all our blessings.

Ezekiel 34:26b
And I will send down the showers in their season; they shall be showers of blessing.

Fixing the Old House

Isaiah 61:4a
They shall build up the ancient ruins, they shall raise up the former devastations.

Psalm 127:1
Unless the LORD builds the house, those who build it labor in vain.

Worn Out

Here I am, Lord,
far removed from the fray,
on our 7th floor balcony.
I see the tops of trees and sky.
Yesterday we all gave out.
Trying to get the old house painted
and cleaned
was too much for us.
Now we have decided to hire the work done.
The walls and ceiling need painting.
We now accept the fact that
the rugs need to be removed
and the floors sanded
in order to sell this house.
The younger generation
does not want wall-to-wall carpeting.
We are out of date, Lord.

Psalm 37:25a
I have been young, and now am old, yet I have not seen the righteous forsaken.

Sorry

Lord, we have now hired painters
to completely paint the inside
of the house. It was too much
for my daughter and me.
The agent said the whole thing
should be done: upstairs, downstairs,
ceilings and all.
I'm sorry we didn't listen sooner
and save ourselves all that work.
Lord, sometimes I should listen
to what others tell me,
but you know it isn't easy.
I'm just glad, Lord,
that others are kind,
and that you take us back,
no matter how foolish we are.
Thank you, Lord,
for love and kindness.

Psalm 36:7
How priceless is your steadfast love, O God! All people may take refuge in the shadow of your wings.

Younger Buyers

Lord, along with downsizing,
we won't show the house again
to potential buyers
for about three weeks.
We've acceded to the realtor's advice
to remove the wall-to-wall carpeting
and have the hardwood floors sanded.
Our realtor says that
buyers will probably be young couples
with both of them working.
They don't have time to fix up a house.
They want to buy one
in perfect condition.
It's hard to be the older generation.
Give us understanding, Lord.

Psalm 71:9
Do not cast me off in the time of old age; do not forsake me when my strength is spent.

To and Fro

O Lord God, we go back and forth
from our apartment to our old house.
This morning we drove to the house.
It didn't sell at our price
so now we are having the rugs taken up
and the floors sanded.
My husband is working on the garage,
I am washing windows again.
Then we go back to our apartment
for dinner. The food is good.
And I don't have to fix it.
We are still getting organized.
There is much to do
both here and there.
We're glad that we moved, Lord,
while we still have the strength
to handle things.

Proverbs 24:3-4
By wisdom a house is built, and by understanding it is established; by knowledge the rooms are filled with all precious and pleasant riches.

On Hold

O Lord our God,
we are waiting for the sanding
and painting to be done
before we put our house
on the market again.
We share our anxiety
about selling the house
with old friends.
and sometimes with new people
we meet in our retirement community.
Everyone is supportive.
When will our house be sold
so that we can be certain
of our situation?
There are so many "if's", Lord.
We rely on your Holy Spirit to hold us up
and lead us through. Amen.

John 14:27
"Peace I leave with you; my peace I give to you. I do not give to you as the world gives. Do not let your hearts be troubled, and do not let them be afraid."

Thursday

Dear Lord, the floor is done
and a new rug
is laid in my husband's study.
The men have gone.
I'm sitting on our swing in the backyard,
perhaps for the last time.
The azaleas and rhododendrons
are blooming.
We have not been able to touch
the garden at our new home.
It is full of weeds,
but it has a nice yellow rose bush.
Maybe this weekend
we will get to it
since our old house
will be shown again.
Lord, bless our houses
and gardens. Amen.

Ecclesiastes 1:4
A generation goes, and a generation comes, but the earth remains forever.

Smoke Detector

My husband is off buying
a new smoke detector for the house, Lord,
before closing on it.
It is amazing the things
that we have let go
without realizing it.
The new people will start fresh
just as we have done in our new apartment.
I wonder how it is with people
who have lived in the same place
for over 50 years.
Most of the people we know
have moved several times
just as we have.
It keeps us on our toes.
You know, Lord, we need reminders
of right living
to keep us from harm.

2 Peter 1:12
Therefore I intend to keep on reminding you of these things, though you know them already and are established in the truth that has come to you.

Tests & Records

Romans 12:2
Do not be conformed to this world, but be transformed by the renewing of your minds, so that you may discern what is the will of God—what is good and acceptable and perfect.

Psychological Test

Dear Lord, I had to have a psychological
test to see if I was all right
to be in our new apartment.
The nurse practitioner
interviewed me.
She rattled off five words
and asked me to remember them.
Then she asked what I would do
if the smoke detector went off
in our apartment
or if there were a fire in the kitchen.
I said, "I would get out."
Then she came back
to the five words.
I could only remember four.
I wondered, Lord,
if this was cause for alarm.
But she said I was OK after all.
I suppose it goes on a record somewhere,
but I'm safe for now.
Are you keeping a record, too, Lord?

Malachi 3:16-17
Then those who revered the LORD spoke with one another. The LORD took note and listened, and a book of remembrance was written before him of those who revered the LORD and thought on his name. They shall be mine, says the LORD of hosts, my special possession on the day when I act, and I will spare them as parents spare their children who serve them.

Records

Today we went to the DMV, Lord,
to get our driver's licenses changed
to our new address
and to register to vote.
What a lot of records
need to be changed
after a move.
We are connected
to so many others
that we don't usually
think about.
Yet, your Spirit
hovers over all
and gives meaning
and purpose to our efforts.

Ecclesiastes 3:1
For everything there is a season, and a time for every matter under heaven.

Dropping the Artillery

O Lord, at night
I take off my pedometer
which registers steps for our health plan.
Then I drop my "Sara", which is the name
given to the health alert monitor
required by our retirement community.
Then I remove my hearing aids,
my glasses, watch,
keys to our building and our room,
my identity card for the dining room
and used tissues I've accumulated.
Then I begin the usual preparations for bed.
You must shake your head
over such an array of artillery
meant to keep us safe and healthy,
when our lives are in your hands, Lord.

Psalm 119:73
Your hands have made me and fashioned me; give me understanding that I may learn your commandments.

Closer to You

Sitting on our apartment balcony
on a fine day, Lord,
I remember the balcony
of our first apartment
after we were married.
From the third floor
we could look down
on the street below.
Here on the seventh floor
we look straight out at trees and sky.
We are closer to heaven
in many ways, such as
I do not have to get meals
and there is less housework
than in a house.
In our first apartment
we barely knew our neighbors.
Here we knew some people before we came
and are getting to know many more.
You have led us all along the way, Lord.
Hold us close as we approach the goal.

Psalm 100:4-5
Enter his gates with thanksgiving, and his courts with praise. Give thanks to him, bless his name. For the LORD is good; his steadfast love endures forever; and his faithfulness to all generations.

Physical Fitness

His perspective

Connected to this place, Lord,
is a gym, swimming pool
and several instructors.
An instructor gave me a mini-fitness test.
Could I stand on one leg for a minute?
How many seconds did it take me
to run around an orange cone
ten feet away?
How many times
could I lift an 8 pound weight
in a minute?
How far could I bend over
to touch my toes?
I barely got past my knees.
Lord, I need work.
I'm looking forward
to getting in better shape.

Ephesians 6:10
Finally, be strong in the Lord and in the strength of his power.

Exercise

Her perspective

Gracious God, you know
my husband signed up
for exercises at the fitness center.
I will have to wait.
My back is still sore.
They also have exercise classes
in our building.
I tried it for two days.
I thought it might make me feel better.
Ouch! Now I am worse than before.
Some things can't be rushed.
I shall rest in you.
Gracious God, you give strength
in the early morning watch.
Your presence continues
to hold me up through the day.
Thank you for healing.

Psalm 69:29
But I am lowly and in pain; let your salvation, O God, protect me.

Fitness Test

His perspective

Dear Lord, our new retirement community
puts emphasis on physical fitness.
They had me take a fitness test
for balance and strength.
The chaplain reminded me
that Jesus and his disciples
walked everywhere they went:
even 100 miles from Capernaum to Jerusalem.
My life has been sedentary.
I'll admit to being 20 pounds
(or more) overweight.
Nevertheless, I'm trying.
I walked two miles the other day.
It wore me out, but I slept well that night.
I'm getting instruction on the weight machines.
I've enrolled in exercises in the swimming pool
to give me endurance and discipline.
Lord, may I serve you
with renewed strength.

Psalm 147:10-11
His delight is not in the strength of the horse, nor his pleasure in the speed of the runner; but the LORD takes pleasure in those who fear him, in those who hope in his steadfast love

New Adventures

Isaiah 42:10
Sing to the LORD a new song, his praise from the end of the earth! Let the sea roar and all that fills it, the coastlands and their inhabitants.

An Adventure

Dear Lord, today I had an adventure.
I went for a ride on the shuttle bus.
to visit church friends
who live in the Health Care Center
of our retirement community.
Now that we live here,
I can visit them more often.
There are many activities
that we take part in
to get to know new people,
but I am glad to see
those we knew before coming here.
It brings back memories.
Lord, your care for us
continues in many ways.

1 Peter 5:7
Cast all your anxiety on him, because he cares for you.

Another Adventure

Father, today I went for my first walk
around our retirement complex.
I walked across the street
to one of the other buildings
and sat on a bench
with a canopy over it.
It had rained during the night
and other benches were wet.
Then I came back to our building
and walked out to see our garden.
It was early
and would have been a good time
to weed before the bugs come out.
But that is for another day.
It is good to get around, Father.
My back is better.
It's a beautiful day.

Psalm 118:24 (RSV)
This is the day that the Lord has made; let us rejoice and be glad in it.

Hymn: "This Is the Day"

Old Friend

Dear Lord,
Our friend from church
is going to move
into our building
in a few months.
It will be good to have her here.
Perhaps we will need to make adjustments
to living so close to each other,
but she has lived in other countries
and is very independent.
I expect she will soon be
the life of the party.
Thank you, Lord, for friends.

Proverbs 17:17a
A friend loves at all times.

Responsibility

Now, Lord of All, our friend,
who is moving into our building,
has asked us to be responsible for her cat,
in case she is moved to a higher care building
where cats are not allowed.
We have resisted efforts
by our grown children
to adopt a cat.
Now, we are signed up, just in case.
Please don't let anything
happen to our friend.
We really don't want a cat.
When we expressed this,
our friend thought our reason
for wanting her well-being was flawed.
Lord of All, you mentioned
care for birds, but what about cats?
A little humor is called for.

Proverbs 18:24
Some friends play at friendship but a true friend sticks closer than one's nearest kin.

Attitude

When I was growing up
we called people in wheelchairs "crippled."
Now that term is no longer acceptable.
When we go to dinner
in our retirement complex, Lord,
we are surrounded
by people in wheelchairs zooming around
and people using walkers.
We have to be careful
not to bump into each other.
Rather than being put off
by these mechanical aids,
your love for all of your children
lets us see beyond the aids
to the valuable person.
You show us the way, Lord.

Luke 12:6-7
"Are not five sparrows sold for two pennies? Yet not one of them is forgotten in God's sight. But even the hairs of your head are all counted. Do not be afraid; you are of more value than many sparrows."

Acceptance

Dear Lord, we are in a caring place.
When I see couples coming to dinner
and one of the two is physically disabled,
either using a wheelchair or walker,
I wonder if this could be us
in a few years.
Then there are those
with mental incapacities.
It takes a bit of getting used to, Lord.
It must have been wonderful,
when you touched people
and made them well.
I wish I could do that.
But making contact
with the real person
is healing, in a way,
for both of us.
Thank you for leading the way.

Matthew 4:23
Jesus went throughout Galilee, teaching in their synagogues and proclaiming the good news of the kingdom and curing every disease and every sickness among the people.

Triumphs

Meeting so many people
who are in our age group
and hearing their stories,
I begin to realize
that no one's life is perfect.
Almost all have lost their parents
and some have lost children
or grandchildren or have had
other tragedies. Being rich
or famous doesn't make one
invulnerable. Lord, we all
need you in our lives
to feel valued and special.
It is wonderful
to live in this community
where people have overcome
to lead joyful lives
in your Spirit.

John 16:33
"I have said this to you, so that in me you may have peace. In the world you face persecution. But take courage; I have conquered the world!"

Stories

When we go to dinner, Lord,
we get to know new people
and learn the stories
of their lives: scientists,
doctors, artists, ministers,
musicians, school teachers,
accountants, and other occupations.
We hear about children,
grandchildren, and great grandchildren.
Then there are the activities
that people take part in here.
And many have exciting travels
to talk about.
We get to tell our stories, too.
There is never a lack
of conversation.
Thank you, Lord,
for your wonderful world
and the great diversity of experience.

Psalm 36:5
Your steadfast love, O LORD, extends to the heavens, your faithfulness to the clouds.

Getting Settled

Numbers 33:53
You shall take possession of the land and settle in it, for I have given you the land to possess.

Disoriented

O Father, after several weeks
in our new home,
where I meet
and talk with new people,
I am now returning
to our church
to meet with my circle.
It's disorienting.
I am neither here nor there.
Help me to keep things straight, Father.
You are with me in both places.
I rely on your continuing presence.

Psalm 73:23
Nevertheless I am continually with you; you hold my right hand.

Hymn: "Trust and Obey"

The Bird Bath

Our daughter gave us the bird bath, Lord.
We couldn't leave it at our old house.
Our grandson helped move it
because it is so heavy.
He is 24, and picked it up easily.
Now we have it in the garden
at our apartment.
My husband fills it
with the hose from a nearby faucet.
The birds come and drink and bathe in it.
We enjoy watching them.
We thank you for the wonders
of your creation.

Genesis 1:20
And God said, "Let the waters bring forth swarms of living creatures, and let birds fly above the earth across the dome of the sky."

Our Garden of Eden

Lord, our garden plot
has been dug up.
We have to hoe it, rake it,
and put in plants and seeds.
We brought the humming bird feeder
and long pole from which it hangs
from our old garden.
We hope it will attract some birds.
My husband found a block of wood
on which to install our sun dial.
Our garden will be our Eden
in the midst of civilization.
Thank you, Lord.

Genesis 2:15
The LORD God took the man and put him in the Garden of Eden to till it and keep it.

Our Bench

O Lord, we couldn't leave the bench
in our old garden.
We needed it to sit on in our new garden.
The bench is old and weather-worn,
but it is perfect for sitting in the garden.
It just fit in the back seat of the car
as we moved it to its new location.
We enjoy it as a place to rest
between planting and weeding,
and just to sit and look at the garden.
You enjoyed being in a garden
with your disciples.
Gardens remind us of your creative presence.
Thank you, Lord, for gardens.

John 18:1
After Jesus had spoken these words, he went out with his disciples across the Kidron valley to a place where there was a garden, which he and his disciples entered.

Looking Ahead

Now someone on our floor
is moving to assisted living.
Two friends are in high level care.
Is that ahead for us, Lord?
Please let my end be swift and clean.
Don't let me linger.
in some somnolent state.
I look forward to being with you, Lord,
in a new exciting place.
Let me live fully until the end,
and then enjoy even greater life
fully in your presence.
Thank you, Lord,
for understanding.

John 14:2-3
"In my Father's house there are many dwelling places. If it were not so, would I have told you that I go to prepare a place for you? And if I go and prepare a place for you, I will come again and will take you to myself, so that where I am, there you may be also."

Caring for Others

Lord, the Caregivers Group
that I joined here
has assigned me
a person to visit
who has recently moved
from an apartment
to assisted living.
I look forward
to ministering
in your name.
Without your life and Spirit
I wouldn't be doing this.
What a difference
you make in our lives
and in the world, Lord.
Though you lived in a small country
long ago and far away,
our lives are changed
as we are led by your Spirit. Amen.

Romans 8:28
We know that all things work together for good for those who love God, who are called according to his purpose.

Rediscovery

Sitting on a bench
near the pond
in our retirement community,
I look around and see
a tiny orange flower
in the grass
and remember
discovering such flowers
as a child as I raised my head
from a crying spree
in the grass.
Then such flowers reminded me
of your presence.
Lord, you were with me then
and continue as my companion
as I encounter old age.

Matthew 28:20b
"And remember I am with you always, to the end of the age."

Milestones

Jeremiah 30:19a
Out of them shall come thanksgiving, and the sound of merrymakers.

Coming Through

The sun shines on a big geranium
that my husband gave me
for Mother's Day
and the window boxes of flowers
my daughter installed
on our balcony.
It's 72° with a slight breeze.
We are becoming settled
even if the house isn't sold.
We have resumed former activities
and are enjoying planting our new garden plot.
Your presence, Lord, has brought us through.
We give you thanks and praise.

Isaiah 43:2a
**When you pass through the waters, I will be with you;
and through the rivers, they shall not overwhelm you.**

Hymn: "Through It All"

Contentment

Dear Lord, Our God,
here I sit on the balcony
of our apartment.
It is 75°: a perfect day!
My red geranium
soaks up the sun.
The floor needs sweeping
where petals have dropped,
but I don't know where
the dust pan is.
I know, Lord, I could improvise,
but it is such a good excuse.
We are settling in.
When we go to dinner
we see old friends
and meet new ones.
You hold us up
in the midst of change.

Psalm 89:1
I will sing of your steadfast love, O LORD, forever;
with my mouth I will proclaim your faithfulness to all
generations.

Hymn: "O God, Our Help in Ages Past"

Summer Solstice

Lord, it is already warm at 6 a.m.
Our garden is blooming
with black-eyed Susan and a rose bush
given to my husband for Father's Day,
along with begonias and lilies
which were planted earlier.
Milkweed plant, cosmos, and forget-me-nots
in the middle of pink flowers
were already here.
Iris, moved from our house,
three tomato plants, and sunflowers
are coming along.
Our zig-zag path of bark
is studded with weeds
which had been turned under.
A flock of goldfinch flies by.
We are enjoying your wonderful world, Lord.

Matthew 6:28b-29
"Consider the lilies of the field, how they grow; they neither toil nor spin, yet I tell you, even Solomon in all his glory was not clothed like one of these."

Wedding Anniversary

It's hard to believe
when I look at pictures of our wedding
and remember who we were then
and still are now,
but with more rounded edges.
I shake my head and wonder
where the time has gone—
all those years of striving
for one thing after another—
and then I smile
over all the effort expended
and enjoy the present
in this retirement home
which your servants
have created for us.
Lord, it must take patience
as you wait for our eyes
to open to eternity.

Psalm 141:8a
But my eyes are turned toward you, O God, my LORD; in you I seek refuge.

John 17:3
"And this is eternal life: that they may know you, the only true God, and Jesus Christ whom you have sent."

Hymn: "Open My Eyes, That I May See"

Big Storm

O LORD of All,
as we drove to our unsold house
from our retirement home,
we saw trees down everywhere.
We were to meet Diane
to arrange for a sale
of all the household goods
that are left.
She arrived late
due to all the trees
blocking the roads.
It gave us time to rake the yard
of twigs and leaves
and haul large branches to a pile
in the back.
O LORD of All, such storms
remind us that we are not in charge.

Luke 8:25b
They were afraid and amazed, and said to one another, "Who then is this, that he commands even the winds and the water, and they obey him?"

Hymn: "Majesty, Worship His Majesty"

4ᵗʰ of July

The rockets' red glare
on the television this year
was a poor substitute
for the usual celebration
in the park.
Trees down and branches everywhere
in the Washington, D.C. area
from the storm You sent
took the efforts of all the city workmen,
so they put off fireworks.
And people say that our country
is getting hotter every year.
What is the meaning of all this weather, Lord?
We look to you for answers.

Psalm 86:7
In the day of my trouble I call on you, for you will answer me.

A Birthday

Dear Lord,
our daughter's birthday is today.
We will celebrate it
in this new place.
I've made the lasagna
and cookie cake she likes.
I have to find the good dishes.
I haven't used them yet.
The movers put things
in logical places,
but not necessarily
where I would put them.
It's fun to get them out again.
The party will be almost normal.
Thank you, Lord, for our daughter
and celebrations that tie us together
and give continuity.

Psalm 69:30
I will praise the name of God with a song; I will magnify him with thanksgiving.

Psalm 133:1
How very good and pleasant it is when kindred live together in unity!

Closing

Psalm 107:1
O give thanks to the **LORD,** for he is good; for his steadfast love endures forever.

Sold Our House

Hallelujah, Dear Lord!
We've sold our house!
After three months
and more than forty lookers
we received an offer we can accept.
We did what the realtor told us:
removed the carpet, refinished the floors,
painted all the walls and woodwork.
Yet no immediate offer.
He concluded that our backyard
with its azaleas and towering trees,
turned out to be a negative.
Young couples want grassy open
space for their children.
In contrast our grandson,
who came to our house every day
after elementary school,
enjoyed tramping through the bamboo jungle,
building a tree house, digging a fish pond
leaping out on a rope swing. Creativity!
But it's not for us to decide
how a new family wants to live.
We're just grateful that the house is sold and
that we'll have the money to pay off the interim loan
for our retirement home.
Thank you, Lord.

Psalm 146:1-2
Praise the LORD! Praise the LORD, O my soul! I will praise the LORD as long as I live; I will sing praises to my God all my life long.

On the Swing Again

One last time—sitting on the swing—
writing in this garden of trees and bushes,
at our old house,
a refuge from the world,
where nature quiets
sounds of distant industry,
birds chirp, insects buzz,
and sunshine patches the ground.
Your presence hallows the space.
How I shall miss being undisturbed,
alone with you, Lord,
Our new space has benches
in quiet places,
but with people walking by.
Lord, open my heart and mind
to new ways
of being in your peace. Amen.

Exodus 33:14
He said, "My presence will go with you, and I will give you rest."

Transition

O Lord, now several weeks after our move,
back at former house
I watch men pack the things
for which we don't have room.
They will go to an auction house.
What a lot we accumulated
that will now be redistributed to others:
the guest room furniture,
the punch bowls, soup tureen and so much more
that we loved to use with company.
I hope the future owners
enjoy all these things
as much as we did.
In our retirement home
we eat with new people everyday
and share food in a buffet or served to us.
It's transition time from old to new ways.
Lord, you are the glue that holds all together.

Psalm 136:1
O give thanks to the LORD, for he is good, for his steadfast love endures forever.

Clean Out

Guest room furniture,
lawn mower, books, vases,
Thai puppets, Japanese umbrellas,
doilies and pictures,
which are without places
in our new apartment
in a retirement community,
will go on auction
and will be picked up today.
Pillows, shovels,
tablecloths, and odd Jello molds
are released from our care.
These things were part
of a full life.
Thank you for their use.
Now, Lord, it's time
to cut down on things and simplify.
Fill us with the riches
of your Spirit.

Ephesians 3:16-17a
I pray that, according to the riches of his glory, he may grant that you may be strengthened in your inner being with power through his Spirit, and that Christ may dwell in your hearts through faith.

Victory Swim

O Gracious Lord, we went for a swim
in the afternoon
in our retirement community pool
to celebrate closing on the house.
Alleluia! Amen!
We are so glad to have it settled
and done—no further improvements
to take care of.
Lord, you know how it has weighed on us
to finish the last details,
clean the house,
and tidy the yard.
It gives us a settled feeling,
like we really live in our apartment now,
and not in a motel.
Thank you for holding us up
all along the way.
Alleluia! Amen!

Psalm 147:1
Praise the LORD! How good it is to sing praises to our God; for he is gracious and a song of praise is fitting.

Hymn: "Come, Christians, Join to Sing"

Settled

Again and again we say,
"Now we are settled."
Two weeks ago
my husband hung the last picture.
A week ago
I started reviewing books again.
Yesterday my husband bought
a humidifier and installed it.
Lord, we have been here six months,
our friend has been here one month.
We feel like old timers.
We have joined
various activities.
We have gotten to know
many other people.
You have been with us
every day as we combine
old and new.

Matthew 13:52
And he said to them, "Therefore every scribe who has been trained for the kingdom of heaven is like the master of a household who brings out of his treasure what is new and what is old."

Thanksgiving

We will be at our daughter's
for Thanksgiving this year, Lord.
We will bring a side dish,
and my daughter will send
some turkey home with us.
But it's not the same
as roasting the turkey
and looking forward
to turkey soup.
Am I missing the point, Lord,
the giving of thanks?
We are thankful for our family
and for this retirement home,
where we look forward
to living out our days
in peace and security
among friendly people.
Thank you, Lord,
for all our blessings.

Psalm 107:21
Let them thank the LORD for his steadfast love, for his wonderful works to humankind.

Hymn: "Now Thank We All Our God"

Christmas Changes

Lord Jesus the celebration
of your birthday is coming.
In our new home
we are not allowed
to have real trees.
My husband and I
shopped for an artificial tree
with the lights already on.
We are not allowed
to have lighted candles,
but we have battery lighted
votary candles
which our daughter
gave us a few years ago
as a joke.
In spite of such changes
we will celebrate
the light of your presence
among us. Come Lord Jesus.

John 1:14
And the Word became flesh and lived among us, and we have seen his glory, the glory as of a father's only son, full of grace and truth.

New Year's Day

Dear Lord, on our first New Year's Day
in the retirement community
we think back over the past year
with gratitude for your steadfast love.
And what a year it's been:
Choosing an apartment, selecting a realtor,
downsizing, stirring up memories,
preparing our house to show,
getting out of the way of lookers,
packing, moving, unpacking,
finally selling our house,
settling in at our new place,
making new friends,
experiencing new adventures.
Every step of the way
your goodness and mercy
followed us as we moved
to our promised land.
For this we are eternally grateful,
O Lord, our sustainer and redeemer.

Psalm 23.6
Surely goodness and mercy shall follow me all the days of my life.

Scriptures Cited
(NRSV unless noted)

Genesis 1:1 (KJV) Creating Order	47
Genesis 1:20 The Bird Bath	110
Genesis 2:15 Our Garden of Eden	111
Genesis 3:8a Gardens	49
Genesis 12:1 It's Not So Far	13
Genesis 12:4b Moving	55
Genesis 13:18 Moved In	67
Genesis 15:15 Spare Me	19
Exodus 23:20 Preparations	21
Exodus 33:14 On the Swing Again	130
Numbers 6:24-26 Choosing an Apartment	17
Numbers 33:53 Getting Settled	107
Deuteronomy 2:7a Cleaning Out the Garage	27
Deuteronomy 33:27 Downsizing	24
2 Samuel 22:29 Health Concerns	6
Job 12:13 Anxious	29
Job 28:12 Neither Here nor There	31
Psalm 9:10 Backyard Cathedral	15
Psalm 16:11 Lightening the Load	26
Psalm 23:1-3 Continuous Care	12
Psalm 23:4a Looking Forward	14
Psalm 23:6 New Year's Day	137
Psalm 25:2a Picking a Place	16

Psalm 31:3 Hesitation	4
Packing	59
Psalm 36:5 Stories	106
Psalm 36:7 Sorry	80
Psalm 37:7a Still Waiting	38
Psalm 37:25a Worn Out	79
Psalm 40:1 Neither Here nor There	31
Psalm 46:1 Anxious	29
Psalm 48:14 Hesitation	3
Psalm 69:29 Exercise	94
Psalm 69:30 A Birthday	125
Psalm 71:9 Younger Buyers	81
Psalm 73:23 Disoriented	109
Psalm 86:7 4th of July	124
Psalm 89:1 Contentment	120
Psalm 95:2, Day 2 In Our Apartment	70
Psalm 100:4-5 Closer to You	92
Psalm 107:1 Closing	127
Psalm 107:21 Thanksgiving	135
Psalm 118:24 (RSV) Another Adventure	100
Psalm 119:27 Creating Order	47
Psalm 119:73 Dropping the Artillery	91
Psalm 119:96 Not Perfect	35
Psalm 127:1 Fixing Old House	77
Psalm 127:3 Breaking the News	11
Psalm 133:1 A Birthday	125

Scriptures Cited

Psalm 136:1 Transition	131
Psalm 139:9-10 Moving Soon	46
Psalm 141:8a Wedding Anniversary	122
Psalm 143:5 Letting Go	28
Psalm 146:1-2 Sold Our House	129
Psalm 147:1 Victory Swim	133
Psalm 147:7-8 Gentle Rain	51
Psalm 147:10-11 Fitness Test	95
Proverbs 17:17a Old Friend	101
Proverbs 18:24 Responsibility	102
Proverbs 24:3-4 To and Fro	82
Proverbs 27:9a Scent	36
Ecclesiastes 1:4 Thursday	84
Ecclesiastes 3:1 Records	90
Ecclesiastes 3:11 Preparing the House	25
Song of Solomon 2:12 Procession	53
Isaiah 26:3 (KJV) Aches and Pains	52
Isaiah 30:15a Moving Day Tomorrow	60
Isaiah 40:31a Still Waiting	38
Isaiah 42:10 New Adventures	97
Isaiah 43:2a Coming Through	119
Isaiah 61:11 Spring Fever	40
Isaiah 61:4a, Fixing Old House	77
Jeremiah 30:19a Milestones	117
Jeremiah 33:3 Decision Time	1

Lamentations 3:25-26 Change	34
Ezekiel 34:26b Tuesday	76
Malachi 3:6 Realtor's Advice	23
Malachi 3:16-17 Psychological Test	89
Matthew 4:23 Acceptance	104
Matthew 6:19-21 Loaned Treasures	39
Matthew 6:26a Bird Feeders	63
Matthew 6:28b-29 Summer Solstice	121
Matthew 11:28 Survival Mode	30
Matthew 13:52 Settled	134
Matthew 14:23 Places for Prayer	20
Matthew 26:6-7 Scent	36
Matthew 26:36 Gardens	49
Matthew 28:20b Moving Day	61
Rediscovery	115
Mark 1:35 Places for Prayer	20
Mark 6:7-9 Second Thoughts	7
Mark 6:31 Quiet Time	48
Mark 6:42-44 Eating Out	74
Mark 10:25 April 1, Waiting	50
Luke 8:24 Our Canoe	64
Luke 8:25b Big Storm	123
Luke 10:27 Saying, "Good-bye"	62
Luke 12:6-7 Attitude	103
Luke 12:25-26 Worry! Worry! Worry!	33

Scriptures Cited

Luke 12:27 Flowers	37
Luke 14:28 Signed Up	43
John 1:14 Christmas Changes	136
John 12:26 New Opportunity	18
John 14:2-3 Looking Ahead	113
John 14:27 On Hold	83
John 16:13 Let's Move	3
John 16:33 Triumphs	105
John 17:3 Wedding Anniversary	122
John 18:1 Our Bench	112
Acts 2:17 Signing Up	45
Acts 2:38 Our Canoe	64
Acts 14:16-17 Satisfied	73
Romans 4:13 Where to Go	9
Romans 8:26 Helpless	75
Romans 8:28 Caring for Others	115
Romans 8:37-39 Presence	65
Romans 12:2 Tests & Records	87
Romans 12:12 Patience	5
1 Corinthians 12:26 More Aches and Pains	58
1 Corinthians 13:4-8a The Big Decision	8
2 Corinthians 13:11 Reorganization	78
Ephesians 3:16-17a Clean Out	132
Ephesians 6:10 Physical Fitness	93
Philippians 4:8, 1st Day New Apartment	69

Hebrews 13:5-6, Monday   57
James 1:17 (KJV), Spring Gifts   41
1 Peter 5:7, An Adventure   99
2 Peter 1:12, Smoke Detector   85
1 John 4:13, Moved In   71

Hymns

"Bless This House" Choosing an Apartment	15
"Come Christians, Join to Sing"	
Victory Swim	129
"God Will Take Care of You" Moved In	71
"Great Is Thy Faithfulness" Anxious	29
"Holy, Holy, Holy! Lord God" (verse 4)	
Presence	65
"How Firm a Foundation" (verse 2) Monday	57
"In the Garden" Flowers	37
"Joyful, Joyful, We Adore Thee" Gentle Rain	51
"Lead On, O King Eternal" Packing	59
"Leaning on the Everlasting Arms"	
Moving Day	61
"Leave It There" Survival Mode	30
"Majesty, Worship His Majesty" Big Storm	123
"Nobody Knows the Trouble I've Seen"	
1st Day, New Apartment	69
"Now Thank We All Our God"	
Thanksgiving	135
"O God, Our Help in Ages Past"	
Contentment	120
"Open My Eyes, That I May See"	
Wedding Anniversary	122

"Praise God, from Whom All Blessings Flow"
    Eating Out   74
"Spirit of God, Descend upon My Heart"
    Signing Up   45
"This Is the Day" Another Adventure   100
"Through It All" Coming Through   119

Trust and Obey" Disoriented   109
"What a Friend We Have in Jesus"
    Worry! Worry! Worry!   33

Made in the USA
Charleston, SC
31 January 2017